MAKE HIM WORSHIP YOU

HOW TO MAKE A MAN WANT YOU, MORE THAN YOU WANT HIM

(REVISED AND EXPANDED)

ATEWO LAOLU-OGUNNIYI

MAKE HIM WORSHIP YOU

Copyright © ATEWO LAOLU-OGUNNIYI 2019

Book Design & Published by:
Emphaloz Publishing House
www.emphaloz.com
publish@emphaloz.com

DEDICATION

I dedicate this book to my parents Laolu and Omolola Ogunniyi.

To my father (Laolu-Ogunniyi) for instilling confidence in me and letting me understand from a young age, that you can achieve anything as long as you set your mind to it.

To the loving memory of my mother (Omolola Laolu-Ogunniyi) who taught me how to listen and communicate deeply and also taught me everything I know about relationships today.

TABLE OF CONTENTS

INTRODUCTION

(A must read)

Would you like to be many steps ahead of a guy who shows interest in you, so you already know his true intentions before he even opens his mouth?

Are you tired of rolling with a guy, starting to really like him, and all of a sudden without a warning he just switches up on you.

You must be tired of how unpredictable a guy's behavior can be, don't you wish to turn the tables?

Maybe you are even married or in a serious relationship, but your man is not as romantic as when you both started dating?

Or maybe you want him to commit and take your relationship seriously?

If it's any of the above, then you have just picked up the right book.

You are about to read one of the greatest and most straightforward books on Male psychology - NO BULLSHIT!

Nonye is the most wife material woman ever. She depicts submissiveness and respect for whoever her partner is. She has been brought up to be a supportive woman to her man. She was told that this is a strength a lot of girls lack, but anytime she shows this good side of her to a man, they simply take it for granted. It now seems to her that this wife-material character is more of a weakness than it is a strength.

Abidemi, just moved to Abuja, to continue her personal business, the stress of living in Lagos was getting too much for her. She has been told that men in Abuja are calmer than the guys in Lagos. However, after a year of settling in Abuja, she has come to the popular conclusion that - all men, everywhere, want the same thing - SEX!

Martha, a 29 year old woman living in Lagos narrates, that her husband's attitude has drastically changed since they got married in 2017. He still performs his husband-duties, providing for her and their new born, but that's where it stops.

It just seemed he was no longer the guy she courted for 4 years, who was all so romantic and caring. Now he was robotic and mechanical about their precious love life. Whenever she complains, the older women tell her to take heart and focus on the child they are raising.

There are millions of Nonyes, Abidemis and Marthas out there, finding it hard to understand the emotional behavior of men.

Why does it appear that it's the ladies who always seem to be on the receiving end (emotionally) in a relationship?

Why is it that it's the woman who is eager to make the relationship better?

It is the woman who puts in effort so they can communicate better as couple.

She's the one who always has to push her boyfriend or even husband into TALKING about issues between both of them. Even times when he is the one at fault, she still has to initiate the conservation to iron-out misunderstandings.

In many marriages, it is often the wife who suggests that she and her husband go for counselling.

You have been given so much advice on how to treat a man, how to make him stay and not look outside, but you have not been told what to do, in case you find yourself mistakenly giving all these good behavior to a *fvckboy*.

So here's what I'm going to do with this book, I am going to paint you a picture that would make things much more clearer to you. I'll show you how to handle the situation when the man you're with (or maybe you just started seeing him) gets into this dull emotional zone.

What you are about to read, I have shared with thousands of women, and I have gotten more than 90% success stories as feedback.

Women who were not getting a single call back, women who their WhatsApp messages were being left on 'read' are now getting 11 missed calls from the same guy. They started seeing a whiny side of the same dude who was all nonchalant and bossy in the way he treated them.

A certain lady had her boyfriend bringing flowers to her office. Same man who stopped being romantic, he went to dig out the spark he had for her, from whenever he kept it. As I am writing this book, they are 6 months married.

Let me add that, men are much more predictable than you think, so this thing works in new relationships, long term relationships and even marriages.

Read this book with an open mind, the tactics here work without a doubt. They would only fail you, if you do not apply them as I have shown you.

You are going on a journey of self-discovery. You would better understand how your upbringing influences the decisions you make as an adult woman and you would realize a lot of mistakes you have been making in the dating world.

There are definitely some errors you might have stubbornly made in the past, the times you decided to be color-blind when the red flags came up and you ended up getting heartbroken, we shall discuss all those too

Now we're going to digest this book in 2 parts.

Part 1 tells us why both men and women date the way they do. This is a very important part of the book, because to know where we are going, we have to know where we are coming from.

We have to look at what makes men and women tick, how parents, society and culture has wired individuals over the years

Part 2 is action packed. This is where I show you how to take charge asap. Here I take you deeper into the mindset of men and show you how to stay one step ahead of them always.

No time! Let's get started!

PART ONE
WHERE WE'RE COMING FROM

If you do not understand your history,
you cannot dictate your future
- Atewo Laolu-Ogunniyi

CHAPTER 1

GIRL!!! WHY ARE YOU LIKE THIS!?!

If you don't like something, change it,
If you can't change it, change your attitude
- Maya Angelou

Girl why are you like this? That's not me asking you the question, it's actually you asking yourself. I just helped you type it out.

Every-time you find yourself in the same damn situation again, being taken for granted for being too nice and caring towards a guy, you ask yourself the question- Why am I like this?

And it's true. Why are you like this?

As a woman, there are certain reasons why you have been operating in the dating world, the way you do. Let's quickly discuss them

1) The way you were brought up

For so long, the young African girl has been given a lot of advice, on how to handle her male-counterpart.

Generation after generation, she has been handed down the Do's and Don'ts on how to make a relationship work with her male partner.

It seems African parents knew they had raised their boys to be less emotionally answerable, when it came to relationships, so the quick fix later on in life, would be to heap the emotional responsibilities on the girl.

This idea follows the sentiment that, the man has already been saddled with the important role of feeding and providing for the family. If he can deliver on providing material things, then to a large extent, he can be excused for not being emotionally available for his wife (and kids).

But its not only an African thing, it's common in many cultures all across the world. The boys are brought up in a way that prepares them to handle tough decisions in life, and from a young age they are conditioned to be less in tune with their emotions. While the girl child is brought up to be softer and more emotionally aware of her environment, since she would soon be a mother and a wife, and the domesticated part of home-care would rest more on her shoulders.

The world of today has changed a lot though.

Today's adult-woman now realizes that the glorified-male-role of going out to get money for raising the family, is something she can equally do, while she still combines that with the emotional burden of the relationship.

This results in today's woman being more emotional demanding than her mother and aunties were in the days of old.

Male behaviour that women would have overlooked 30 years ago, has become something that women of today do not want to settle for and accept as normal.

For example, 30 years ago it was a common idea among women, to look away when their men flirt with other women. A woman in those times could say "it's okay if her man cheats, as long as he uses protection and he doesn't make her know about it."

Today's woman is now a little torn in between the teachings of her mother's generation and the awareness of her own generation.

This is why it seems a lot of women are indecisive when their man does something intense like 'cheating'.

On one hand she wants to follow the teachings of her mother and aunties, while on the other hand she wants to reason like the modern woman that she is.

2) Pressure from older family members

You need to be careful what advises you take from the older generation and watch how much you allow them to unnecessarily guilt-trip you.

Make sure you are not being rebellious, listen to them with humility because they have some very solid life principles from their time. However, you must also realize that our parents and a lot of people in that generation operate from a low level of emotional intelligence.

I'm sorry I have to scatter this table, but a lot of times when African parents scream on their child to go and marry, it has less to do with the child's growth and happiness and more to do with their own selfish interests as parents.

I have seen hundreds of parents who prefer to nag about how an unmarried daughter is disgracing the family rather than take time to speak with the girl and find out what she might be going through emotionally.

As many of them are so stubborn and unteachable, it means they might be giving you some advises that are only applicable to a world that doesn't exist anymore.

In the 1980's if a woman wasn't married by the age of 29/30, she would start feeling ashamed of herself, but nowadays, there are many single 30 something year old single-women, who are doing very well for themselves.

In your generation, a man isn't the price anymore, BUT a lot of girls are still praying for their Prince Charming to show up. This is partly because the pressure young girls are getting from their mothers, fathers aunties and older relatives is much.

Of course, the idea is to get married and start a family, but this doesn't mean you should tie the right knot with the wrong person, just because society is watching (Half of society don't even know what they themselves are doing anyway)

Omolere, a 33 year old working class lady, dreads going to her family house. She gets worked up whenever there is a family function that requires her to come in contact with her old uncles and aunts.

Even though she has a great job, and she's doing well for herself, her family members make her feel bad just because she hasn't brought a man home yet. This drains her emotionally!

With this type of external pressure from people whom you call your loved ones, it explains why many women of marriageable age sometimes find it hard to walk out of a toxic relationship. Especially when her family members have met the man she plans to marry.

It becomes more about 'what-people-will-say' than it is about the girl's happiness and emotional health.

Let me give you another example of how parents pressure their daughters into making faulty relationship decisions.

A while ago, a lady told me how she was scared of going into marriage with her fiancé. They had started hitting each other physically and they just weren't seeing eye to eye. I advised her to speak with her man and they should consider pushing the marriage forward.

If they were deeply keen on marrying each other, they should go for pre-marital counselling, as there was hope that they could just get it right before taking one of the most important decisions of their life.

When her mother heard what the young lady was contemplating, the mother knelt down and begged her not to postpone the wedding as it would disgrace their family.

3 years later, this lady and her husband are no longer sleeping in the same room in the house. They've had sex less than 5 times in those 3 years, and one of it led to the birth of their son. When she got pregnant, she and her husband even grew apart the more, he treated her with more disdain than ever.

At this point the only thing her mother had to say to her is- "Take heart, that is how marriage is".

Your Nature, your instincts

As we are talking about social and cultural influences on a person, we cannot leave out HUMAN NATURE.

Even though we tend to act like we always know what we are doing, our Human nature is often running the show behind the scenes.

Your natural instincts as a woman also have a role to play in how you handle relationships.

Women are more emotional than men. This is not a good thing or a bad thing. It is just a thing.

Depending on the situation, it can either be a strength or a weakness.

God must have had reasons for making it this way, probably because it is inevitable, a woman is going to be more physically close to a new born baby (breastfeeding and all) than the man, so she is equipped with the softness and compassion to cope with nurturing such fragile and young life.

Every human being has some characteristics of the opposite sex. Men have a feminine side, while women also have a masculine side. However, I can personally say 85% of women are feminine women, which is a beautiful thing.

This means that you live your best life when you're with a man who allows you to be true to your nature. A man who makes it easy for you to express your feminine strengths and at the same time be womanly-soft in his presence.

The wrong man could capitalize on this, and use his masculine qualities to emotionally bully the woman. As she caves in more into her soft feminine nature, she can go from being submissive to totally losing her voice in the relationship.

This is why, a woman who is in a relationship with a boyfriend or husband that's emotionally manipulative, has more heartaches than the lucky lady who has a good-loving man.

CHAPTER 2

WHY DO MEN BEHAVE LIKE THIS?

When a man teaches his son,
he also teaches his son's son
- The Talmud

For you to have picked up this book, it means you are interested in dating, and not only do you want to date, you also want a DRAMA-FREE RELATIONSHIP.

But then it's not easy to start a relationship, if the men in your generation are usually un-serious when it comes to committing and it's not easy to keep a peaceful relationship if many of the men you get to meet are drama kings.

My mission with this book is to help you be on top of your game! I'll show you how to make your man worship you, just the way you want. Your sanity is what I'm interested in here.

This is why you need to allow me tell you about the men in your generation. I'm guessing the generation of men, who you want to pick a partner from, is one of the generations born between the years 1970-2000.

If I'm right, then it's important to know how the men in this generation were brought up and the type of home training they received from their Fathers, Mothers and the society.

There are 4 important things I want you to know about the men in your generation. I'm not stating these points below as excuses for these men but rather I want us to analyse the male behavior in detail.

These 4 important points are (1) He Hides His Emotions (2) His Beliefs Are Patriarchal (3) His Freedom Means A Lot to Him (4) His Mentors Are Polygamous in Nature

1) HE HIDES HIS EMOTIONS

The men in your generation were brought up to believe that men don't show emotions. It was seen as anti-masculine for a man to be all mushy and romantic. This way of thinking made young boys grow up, hiding their emotions.

We all know that what a person repeatedly does, becomes a habit. These young boys grew up, always hiding their emotions, and now that they are grown men, they are not aware of those emotions anymore. The emotions are buried deep down where he hides the little boy in him.

So, it's not that he doesn't have emotions, as a matter of fact, he has loads of emotions, the only thing is- HE IS NOT REALLY AWARE OF THESE EMOTIONS ANYMORE.

But these emotions are still there, and when they are tapped, they are very much as active as when he was 3 years old. If you want him to treat you good the way you want, then you simply need to know when to awaken these emotions and when to quieten them

There is nothing like 'a man who doesn't feel emotions' even Napoleon Bonaparte, who was the greatest war general of all time, was highly emotional. His last word on his dying bed, was JOSEPHINE (his wife's name)

Now, I know you might be thinking "Why should I be the one to study a man's emotional set-up, why can't he study mine".

Remember, this book is for you (the woman) - to learn how to get the best out of your relationships and love life.

I just mentioned above, that all their life, men have been conditioned to repress their emotions, to the point that they no longer know how to deeply feel and access them. Is that the person that you want to wait for to understand your emotions? Someone that does not even understand himself?

My sister, take charge of your love life! Stop living life being uncertain of how one man is going to treat you.

2) HIS BELIEFS ARE PATRIARCHAL

Let's imagine a group of kids playing in two groups. 3 girls in one group and 3 boys in the other group.

One group is playing football outside, jumping, screaming and getting dirty, while the other group is in the house playing with dolls, wearing aprons and acting like chefs in the kitchen.

Which activities do you think the 'boy group' is doing? The boys are the ones indoors, playing with dolls, and acting as cooks in the kitchen - right?

Oh - wrong?

Yes, your guess was the same as mine. The boys are the ones outside playing football, while the girls are the ones indoors with the dolls.

Of course, there are little girls, who like to play football just like the boys, and there are boys who might play with dolls too, but I'm speaking of the most-common-scenarios here.

Now you see, all of us have it heavily engraved in our subconscious that there are some things that boys do, while there are somethings that girls do.

This is the BELIEF that I am talking about. We all have certain things that we have accepted all through our life. The men in your generation have certain phrases that have been heavily drummed into their brains and have now formed a great part of their belief system.

Some examples are-

THE MAN IS THE HEAD OF THE HOUSE.

A WOMAN SHOULD BE SUBMISSIVE TO HER HUSBAND AT ALL TIMES

THE MAN MUST BE THE PROVIDER FOR HIS FAMILY

MEN ARE POLYGAMOUS BY NATURE

THE WOMAN IS MORE RESPONSIBLE FOR GIVING THE CHILDREN HOME-TRAINING

A MAN MUST PAY BRIDE PRICE BEFORE HE CAN MARRY HIS GIRLFRIEND

Now the world has changed a lot from the times we were brought up, civilization has given the female gender more avenues to express herself, but guess what- These beliefs are still heavily embedded in our minds, and every day they influence how most of us behave in our relationships.

3) HIS FREEDOM MEANS A LOT TO HIM

Men in your generation, enjoyed much more freedom growing up than the girls did. Parents were more strict with the girls.

Daughters were drilled on lessons of etiquette and self-composure, while the boys were let loose on many issues. This followed the dominant social values of past centuries when it was believed that the boy would grow to be the head of the family, and he would need to always be out there hustling to provide bread for his family.

Now the definition of 'hustle' has changed a lot over the last 4 decades, a lot more women are now out there 'hustling' to also get bread for the family. But despite the fact that times have changed, the social engineering with which we were brought up, remains deep in our subconscious.

A guy might have slept with 100 girls before he finally decides to settle down with one woman, even though his bride might not be willing to always discuss his past, she is secretly happy that she's the one who could tame this bad boy and turn him to a husband material.

Now flip the script, this same bachelor is in search of a bride, and he discovers that a lady he is eyeing has slept with 50 men, he probably wouldn't want to proceed in making her a bride. He would feel like, marrying her means he is the one carrying a lady that has been used by other men.

Don't frown yet, because even women perpetuate this way of thinking, it's not only the men. The issue of body count is still a big deal in the world of women, whereas guys feel the more girls they sleep with, the more it proves their manliness.

This shows us that men enjoy a large degree of SEXUAL FREEDOM all their growing years, and when he sees that a committed relationship is going to put a stop to this 'sexual freedom', he starts hesitating about taking the relationship to the next level.

There is no male word for 'WHORE'. If there is, it's quite ineffective, or maybe it even makes guys feel cool all the more when they are called such title e.g., 'PLAYER'

Growing up with this much freedom, we can see why a man feels threatened when he realizes that a committed relationship means he can't flirt around the opposite sex, as freely as he used to do before.

4) HIS MENTORS ARE POLYGAMOUS IN NATURE

I interviewed over 500 men in the writing of this book. Not up to 10% of them confirmed that their father or any of their uncles ever gave them a lecture on the importance of staying with one woman. As a matter of fact, uncles and older men in the society always made it look cool to be having extra-marital affairs.

A lot of men in your generation grew up hearing their grandmother tell their mum that, she shouldn't complain if her husband cheated, as long as he doesn't bring these other girls home to her. Cheating was treated like an accepted male trait.

A lot of men in your generation have been hard wired this way and they're not trying to move with the times. Many still want their wife to behave like they are in 1974, but times have really changed.

In my upcoming book for the men, I break it down for guys how they can get maximum happiness from treating their woman the way she wants to be treated. Stubbornly hanging on to the way our fathers treated our mothers is not going to favor anybody. Most women just want a happy home with mutual respect and open communication. In my opinion, that is not too much to ask for.

PART TWO
TAKING CHARGE!!!

*"I would rather you are a creator of circumstance,
than a creature of circumstance"*
-Benjamin Disraeli

CHAPTER 3

IS HE CHANGING?

"Change is a constant thing,
In an indecisive man's behavior"
- Atewo Laolu - Ogunniyi

W hen a man does not know where he is going, and you are emotionally involved with him, it is only normal that you will be dragged along in his inconsistent approach to the relationship that brought both of you together.

Now let's look at your situation.

Has he started making it look like you are the one who is going paranoid?

Is he frequently making it seem like you're over-reacting?

Okay we're there. He is definitely changing!

Someone who used to send you good morning texts, someone who would return your missed call in 0.3 seconds and all of a sudden, he has gone into lean-back mode? I think your instincts are right on this one.

So, this is the most common scenario - You meet a guy, you and him start getting along really well, and all of a sudden, he starts changing.

You just woke up one day, and your sweet puppy has changed color. Wow, this wasn't no puppy all along. This is a chameleon.

The calls reduce, his attention is divided. He makes excuses, and claims that he is busy, or he is just going through some stuff. But as a woman, you naturally have a very strong intuition for people's deeper feelings. You can tell when something is wrong.

You try to stay calm, but you're agitated by the way he acts nonchalant, like everything is okay, when it is obvious that it isn't

When a lot of girls are in situations like this, they really desire to iron issues out, but *the more she attempts to have a decent conservation with him, the more he gets emotionally distant.*

When it comes to 'relationship status' women hate any form of uncertainty. It's either YES or NO. Women hate guessing! And

I know this is the situation you have found yourself now. Maybe this is not even the first time it's happening to you.

THE 4 ZONES OF DATING

There are 4 zones you pass through when you want to date and settle with a guy. Problem starts when you rush past one zone and jump to the other (which is a mistake a lot of women make when love begins to shack them)

The 4 zones are:

- The Friend Zone
- The 'What Are We' Zone
- The Commitment Zone and
- The Proposal Zone

THE FRIEND ZONE - Another name for the friend zone is the MEETING-ZONE. This is when a girl meets a guy and they get talking. There is some level of attraction and they seem to have an interest in each other. The ball is totally in the girl's court here, and she dictates where the relationship goes to next and how fast.

Men are usually of their best behavior while going through the Friend-zone, because no guy wants to get stuck there. So he does everything to impress the girl and to show her he is worthy of a promotion

THE 'WHAT ARE WE' ZONE - This is also called the 'FLING ZONE. Here the ball is not totally in the girl's court any longer. She has flashed him the green light through her actions, and now she's waiting for him to ask her out. (I know we do have some rare occasions, where it's the girl who asks the boy out, but this book is addressing most-common-cases)

This is the stage where a lot of women make mistakes. You're beginning to fall deeper for him, so if any red-flag pops up in your face, you wouldn't look at it twice

Now you're getting to that love-is-blind stage. If he starts showing the symptoms of a fvckboy, your emotions would blind you.

Now he keeps telling you all the sweet words you like to hear and he showers you with attention, at the same time he's making sexual advances.

You are not a robot, you're a human being too, so you simply bring down your defenses and you let him in

THE COMMITMENT ZONE - This is the zone of exclusivity. Here, the relationship has fully begun. No more uncertainties, everyone now knows both of you as boyfriend/girlfriend.

In this zone the ball is not in the guy's court or in the girl's court. It's simply a zone where you have entrusted your hearts to each other.

This is actually the zone where a girl can totally let her guard down and begin to fully invest her all into the relationship.

The mistake is that most women start treating a guy like they are already in the commitment zone, while they were still in the 'what-are-we' zone. If the guy happens to be someone who just wanted sex, it's very easy for the relationship to never get past that 'what-are-we-zone'. *You started giving him the benefits of a boyfriend, without the responsibility of actually being one.* Therefore, he sees no reason in committing further.

THE PROPOSAL ZONE - This is the final stage of the dating phase, where the guy asks the girl - WILL YOU MARRY ME and she says YES! What comes after this is Marriage.

You are reading this book, because you have made the mistake of rushing through the 'what are we' zone and handling the relationship like both of you are already at the 'commitment' zone, only for the guy to remind you that you are the one who has been over assuming things.

Because you were too eager to be in the commitment zone, you had already given him sex, now that he is leaning back, you're getting worried. You don't want to feel like you just had casual sex with just another guy.

The thought of adding another body count and not getting some form of commitment out of it is not palatable to you, so you start getting more clingy, trying to show him you love him, checking up on him, asking how his day went, anything to just prove your love for him.

Naturally he should be the one chasing you, but now the table has turned and suddenly you're the one doing all of the chasing

If you're currently at this point of uncertainty, it is very normal that you would be highly emotional, so I need you to slow down, take a deep breath and think!

There is nothing wrong with you trying to make sense of what you're having with the guy. There is nothing wrong with the fact that you are being emotional, it is your feminine nature, it is what makes you human and it is the reason why you are so entangled to him.

The only issue is that you're the one carrying all the emotional burden, while he just seems to be having fun with the situation

Now you need to realize that - a 'man' can be emotional too and all you have to do is find a way to get a grip on his emotions.

Why does it matter if he gets emotional too?

It matters a lot, because a man's sexual desires can motivate him to participate in a relationship when it's at the Friend Zone and the What-Are-We Zone, but it is mostly when his emotions are involved, that he sits up and works hard to get you and him to the Commitment Zone.

If his emotions are not engaged and involved, and his sexual desires have been satisfied, he easily becomes emotionally stagnant, leaving you to keep doing all the work to keep the relationship on its feet.

CHAPTER 4

YOU ARE THE ONE IN CONTROL

If giving leaves you feeling empty,
You're giving too much
to the wrong person
- Pavana Reddy

There's something you're doing, that's making him feel good and making him take you for granted. YOU ARE BEING TOO NICE AND TOO AVAILABLE!

Little did you know that you have more control of the situation than he does, because you are the one feeding him the emotional food that's making him misbehave. Take away this thing that you're doing that's making him feel over-confident and you would see him for who he truly is.

So how do you go about this?

As a woman you have many many ways you can be moved emotionally, if you watch a very romantic movie, you'll feel like crying, if your sister is getting married, you and your mum can be crying on the wedding day, if you have a child, you might have cried when your baby took his/her first steps.

Being emotional and being able to easily express their emotions just comes naturally to a lot of women, that's why it seems women are more into romance than men.

Men on the other hand are not that emotionally expressive, remember I explained at the beginning of this book that all his life he has being conditioned to push his emotions aside. And not only that, naturally men are not half as hormonal as women, men don't have menstrual periods, PMS and all these things' you women get. These hormonal variations give you more emotional highs and lows than men.

The only hormone in this life, that men have so much more than women is **testosterone,** which is responsible for his large appetite for SEX and that manly thing called EGO.

This is the point I have been waiting to get you to. So when God created women to be emotional, he didn't leave his daughters stranded.

God gave you 2 ways you can bring a man to his senses, two ways by which you can access and make a man emotional. These are:

1) **HIS SEX DRIVE**
2) **HIS EGO**

1. HIS SEX DRIVE: Men have a huge sexual appetite, and society allows men a sexual freedom that makes it easy for them to display their sexual appetite. While some women might still be concerned about having multiple body-counts, a lot of guys take pride in the fact that they have slept with lots and lots of women.

A lot of men also use their sexual adventures to measure how manly they are. The more women he has fussing over him, the more he feels like a stallion. Because of this, men do all sorts of unimaginable things when they want to have sex. He can travel from one country to another, he can spend huge amounts of money, or he can even profess true love to a lady, just so he can get into her pants.

Let me digress a little; I remember a while ago when I entered an uber, the uber driver was a man in his early forties and he recognized me immediately. He said he had been seeing a lot of my relationship talks on social media and that he seriously needed advice.

He narrated a scenario to me, where he dropped 7,000 naira for his wife at home, he now drove 205km from Lagos state to Osun state to see a new chic he just met. He said he spent 2 days with the lady and squandered 90,000 naira (which he told his wife he didn't have). On his way back he felt so stupid and promised never to do such again. Lo and behold a few weeks later he was hunting for a side-chic again. He begged me to teach him how to control his excessive sexual desires. He badly wanted to change, but he just didn't know how to.

He is not the only one, a lot of men do very irrational things when they are horny. SEX IS A VERY POWERFUL MOTIVATOR FOR MEN!

Have you noticed that before you allow a guy to have sex with you, he is so intense, so interested, he calls and checks up on you often. That's because he is thinking with his dick and when men think with their dick, they are so emotional.

All this time, you are still being logical. Even if you're becoming very attracted to the guy, you're still contemplating whether or not you should give him sex yet.

But he is so passionate, and pushful that his persistence, begins to affect you and you start bending your *'NO SEX YET'* rule

Now as soon as both of you have sex, the guy becomes logical and starts thinking with his head again, because his dick has been satisfied, and that's the point when you start been overly emotional.

Now holding sex back and making him wait for it, is a good old trick that works.

In his book *Act Like a Lady, Think Like a Man,* Steve Harvey talks about the '90 DAY RULE'. He explains that ladies should withhold sex from an interested guy, for the first 90 days of meeting him.

The truth is a fvckboy who only wants to get into your pants would not be patient for a whole 90 days. It is very rare. So, this way you get to weed out a lot of guys who don't have good intentions

Most women however, start thinking they could lose a guy because they aren't giving him sex and out of that little panic, they give him the cookie.

It's even possible that you get attracted to a guy real quick, it's being a while you had someone hold you close like this and it feels good and before you think clearly, you have slept with him.

Since all these scenarios are possible, then there has to be another way to get him back into an emotional state. If the sex satisfaction is making him slack off and relax, there must be a way to make him passionate again.

This takes us to the second way of getting a man a emotionally into you - HIS EGO.

2. HIS EGO: When a woman has sensitive tingles in her head, she becomes emotional, but for most guys, it is when they have sexual or egocentric impulses in their brain that they become emotional- very emotional.

Let's talk about these egocentric pulses.

This is your focus now! The 90 Day Rule has failed, you people have already *knacked* each other's brains out and a few orgasms later, he starts to play your emotions against you?

Not so fast, you are the one who is actually going to play his ego, against him.

It's important for you know that egocentric men are the most emotional men on earth.

An egocentric man is not in touch with his emotional side, as a matter of fact, he does not believe that he has an emotional side. It is his ego that tells him this lie, meanwhile, it is within this very ego of his, that all his emotions hide.

This denial of their emotional side, makes most men unaware that these emotions are truly a part of their nature.

You have total control over his egocentric side, because it is the fuss that you are making over him, that he is using to boost his self-esteem. HE IS GETTING HIGH OFF YOU! Remain the sweet woman that you are, but unplug the life-line you have been feeding his ego, and he'll come running right back to mama - YOU!

When a man cannot get a woman under his control, it messes with his head big time. It's a woman's way of clearly communicating to him (without words), that he is not MAN ENOUGH.

So when you are at this stage, strike at his ego with a little dis-interest, then take a step back, and his emotional side would fully reveal itself. And because he is unaware that he has this emotional side in him, he's not going to know what hit him.

CHAPTER 5

WHAT A MAN CAN PLAY, A WOMAN CAN PLAY BETTER!

Treat me like a princess
I'll treat you like a prince,
Treat me like a game
and I'll show you how it's played.
- Anonymous

In my experience as a relationship-coach, I have heard a lot of women say, " Oh I hate playing games, if a guy can't be straight-forward with me, then I am not interested. I can't hide my feelings or do all these childish things e.g not calling him when I feel like, or not expressing my emotions when something is bothering me"

First of all, if you want someone who you're certain would be straight-forward with you all the time, what you need is a puppy dog, not a man.

Human beings are not always straight-forward! Even you, cannot boast that you're always transparent in all your endeavours.

One of my close friends (a newly wedded couple whom I coach), just had a beautiful baby girl. I call her my god-daughter. This 8-month old baby has already mastered the art of manipulation. She knows just when and how to cry when she wants extra attention.

Her mother said she has different crying modes. There's a certain pitch when she's crying out of hunger and she wants to eat. It's a different type of 'cry' when she's crying out of pain or discomfort and still yet another type of cry when there's nothing wrong, but she just wants attention. I'm sure the women who have had a child can testify to this.

Can you just believe it, these tiny toddlers already know how to make other human beings bend to their will.

What point am I trying to make here? I'm just showing you that humans are born with a natural instinct, to always try to manipulate other humans into giving them what they want.

Listen, you cannot be a spectator in your own life. *You need to be a creator of circumstances, not a creature of circumstances.* Common! You are stronger and more powerful than you are showing the world.

Sister, I will remind you who you are, so you can bring your A-game to the table, every-time, every day.

You are in the game already; so play and PLAY GOOD!' As long as you live, you have to deal with other human beings, who have their own personal interests and desires on the table. It's a good feeling to grant the wishes of someone you love, and go the extra mile for them, but it's also essential that you learn how to bring people to order, especially if you're dealing with someone who is self-centred.

Men naturally have an ego. Some men don't know how to control this ego, they could make big life-decisions without knowing their ego is the one controlling them.

Our predominant African culture (and many other cultures across the world) have been highly patriarchal for generations. So this means the man you are dealing with probably has this upbringing and mentality of I-AM-THE-MAN. Being brought up on this side of the world means, a lot of guys believe they can eat their cake and have it, after-all society wouldn't judge him per se.

Having this in mind, means you should learn how to protect yourself and your emotions. Keep being nice, keep being kind, but don't be quick to conclude that you have landed yourself a fairy-tale relationship

You cannot and you should not, start to show a man how much you love and need him, when his manly - ego is still bigger than the love he has for you.

In this game of love, a man can be selfish when he starts off with a woman. He simply looks out for what he wants from her, maybe it's the SEX with her, maybe it's the CONTROL over her, whichever it is, he would try to influence the way things happen between you and him in his favor.

Here's what I mean, when you just start hooking up with a guy, it's very possible that his level of selfishness is still much greater than his level of selflessness.

At this point he is still more into himself, than he is into you, so if you start giving him too much love and attention too early, he might not reciprocate with the same intensity.

He is more interested in personal gains, whereas you are already looking out for both of you's mutual benefits. This is the reason why it seems there's more love-vibes coming from your end, than from his.

So you need to be sure what level your companionship with a guy is, before you start showing all your cards.

We live in an insecure world where everyone is trying to feel good off the other person (unconsciously) and this is where women are mostly victims, because at the beginning of a relationship, out of being the more emotional gender, they tend to skip ahead (emotionally) already dreaming of the *happily ever after.*

Meanwhile the sex has satisfied a major urge for the guy and his initial motivation has dropped from 100% to 10%.

Now as a woman, do NOT to lie to yourself that you already have butterflies in your stomach. What you need to do is hold your breath, hold your emotions. The importance of holding your emotions back a little longer, is to prevent you from hurriedly bending your principles, adjusting your life to accommodate his plans.

He goes days without calling you, then one day he randomly calls that he is coming to pick you up, and because you have been feeling unwanted by him, because you have missed him a lot, you drop everything you're doing and redirect all your plans to suite his.

You're going to stop acting that way now! Don't always be there at his beck and call! I know you miss him, but you have to let him see that you have a life without him.

I am telling you this with all my experience in this relationship-field, there is nothing a man respects more than a woman who he cannot not easily distract. It's a major turn-on for guys.

He enjoys exercising this power over you, when you try and resist, he will quickly burst your head with some sweet words and promises that are not totally binding on him.

My sister, appreciate the attention, blush if you feel like blushing, but still keep your feet firm on the ground. At this point, a lady's heart is already beating fast, you just want to jump into his arms and be his baby girl... KAI! It is not time for you to be falling anyhow.

When he sees that you appreciate the attention but you are NOT going to be totally distracted by it, it makes him want to do more. It doesn't matter if you guys have already had sex a couple of times, you relegate his ass back to the starting line. There is nothing men admire more than a woman who has her personal principles and sticks to it.

I am not saying you should be rigid, rude or inconsiderate, NO! You are just laying down some principles, so he can see that he is dealing with a different type of lady this time - A QUEEN!

When you aren't sure of a guy's true motive yet, it would be unfair to act like you don't see the efforts he is putting in, because you never know if his intentions are for real.

To make this clearer, let me give you an example below:

Let's imagine one of your toasters (suitors), calls you up

Toaster: Hey babe whats up? I wanna come take you out to the movies

(Meanwhile you planned to stay home with your girls and casually gist)

You: Aww, that's nice of you, but I actually planned to stay home today and gist with my friends.

Toaster: Oh, in that case, tell your friend or friends to come along, let me take all of you out

You: No, we actually just wanna be by ourselves tonight.

Toaster: (now wondering I wanna take this girl out to have a nice time, I have it all planned out, but she would rather stay home and be with her friends)

From the above scenario, the guy is going to seriously respect the fact that you stand your ground. He would be blown away by the fact that he could not sway you away from your everyday life.

Even if your girls are not around, and you're home alone, and you are going to be bored, if your instincts have been warning you, that you need to lean back a little, then heed that warning and bring the example we quoted above to life.

I really don't give a shit if some people term this as 'emotional-manipulation'. No problem - let it be emotional manipulation, after-all you're trying to wake him up emotionally in the first place.

Men go extreme lengths when calculating how to win a girl's heart or get into her pants. Do you know how much he calculates and plans every move just to catch you? *I should buy her this, I should buy tell that,* every move is calculated to make you fall for him.

So why do you women think it is absurd to calculate your way into having him behave the way you want?

Is it that you believe it's supposed to happen automatically? Or is it because girls watch too much Cinderella, Little mermaid, Princess and the frog while growing up? Well reality-check, Prince Charming is a playboy these days, his mama spoilt him and society hasn't been judging him, so you have to command respect for yourself so he acts accordingly

I mentioned earlier, that I would rather you are a *creator of circumstances, rather than a creature of circumstances*

Don't let all that 'love is not mathematics' idea, push you into a state of inactivity, I agree that love isn't mathematics, but trust me it sure requires little calculations here and there, if you want to get what you deserve.

They say 'Emotions are feelings in motion' you're a grown woman, you just have to master the timing of when to show your emotions.

It's not really about you being less emotional and more logical - NO! It's more about you learning when to let go and allow your emotional side control you, and when to sit up and let your logical side run the show.

In this world of guy-code and girl-code, no two situations are the same, which is the more reason why you need to apply yourself and your inner game, when you're dealing with a guy

Let's take a quick look at another example below:

If a guy tells you to come to his place and he hints at having sex, if your mind is totally cool with having sex with him at that point in time, then very well - it's your body, go ahead and enjoy yourself.

But if having sex at that point is against your ground rules, then you should not honour his invitation to his place. You wouldn't wait till you are *netflixing and chilling* and his hand is halfway up your thighs before you realize you are a woman with principles, that's going to make you look like you don't have a mind of your own.

Don't excuse yourself by claiming that you didn't expect him to make sexual advances. C'mon you definitely would have seen the signs, if they are there. Let a man see that you are a thinking woman, let him perceive you as a woman with foresight, and that you would not put yourself in a situation that would make you violate your principles.

MEN LOVE CONFIDENT WOMEN. He would try and make it seem like you're childishly playing hard-to-get, but that's all part of the silly mind-games that men play.

If you are not ready to let the relationship move that fast, if you want to take things nice and slow, then calmly communicate that to him with your words or your actions.

He would totally admire your stand, even though he might not say it, but remember he is selfish at the moment, so he would say things to, make it seem like you are been too hard - ANSWER HIM NOT, stand your ground!

CHAPTER 6

DEFLATE HIS EGO

The more you feed a selfish man's ego,
The more he would suffocate
and break your heart
- Atewo Laolu-Ogunniyi

When a guy is interested in having sex with you, he is super motivated by his high level of hornyness, and because of this he would pay attention to everything you tell or ask him. He would remember to call, he would check up on you e.g. How was your day hun? Hey dearie, have you eaten? etc

It is very rare that a man would turn cold before having sex with you; it happens but it's very rare. Most men start to slack off, after they have gotten a taste of the sex.

When a man starts acting funny after having sex with you, you need to relax! DON'T let your emotions start pushing you into a panic. I know what comes to your mind when this happens is that you are worried that your worst nightmare might be coming to pass. You don't want to realize that he is just like the other guys. You would hate to face that disappointment again. I totally understand.

But now you're harboring a sense-of-guilt that is taking over you and driving you to a point where you start calling him over and over again. There is a sudden fear in you, and it's making you drop loads of missed calls on his phone.

When you finally get to talk to him, you try to force him to reason with you, and *the more you push, the more he is going to pull away.* And the more you do this, the more you are caressing and inflating his ego.

If everything you're doing at this point is inflating his ego, then it simply means you should start doing the opposite - DEFLATE HIS EGO.

You need to go back into yourself and find balance. Silence that inner voice that preaches fear, remorse and shame, TELL IT TO SHUT UP! Now increase the volume of that voice that strengthens your inner sense of security. You are not the first woman this is happening to, and mistakenly having sex with a wrong guy is not the end of the world.

A lot of guys are egocentric, and as long as you make yourself overly available, he would keep feeding his ego off your desperation. If you want a man to respect and value you, then you need to give him SPACE and THE SILENT TREATMENT.

I don't know if you have noticed, but he is very happy that he still has control over you. He knows he still has control over you because of the way you desperately try to reach out to him and try to convince him to love you right. Also, you're always ready to go out of your way to link up with him whenever he calls.

The moment a man's sex drive is satisfied, it's not the words you say that he hears. "Oh, but you know I love you" "Why are you changing?" "Talk to me, what is the problem?" All this type of ranting just goes in one ear, and comes out of the other.

IT'S ACTUALLY WHAT YOU DON'T SAY THAT MEN HEAR, YOUR ACTIONS WOULD NOW SPEAK LOUDER THAN YOUR WORDS.

If he thinks because he has had sex, he can run away, allow him that temporary victory -because if you follow the things, I'm teaching you - he would soon come back. Don't let fear-of-the-unknown take over you.

Girl, STAND YOUR GROUND! Don't go after him. I repeat - DO NOT GO AFTER HIM.

After a while, his curiosity would start pinching him, and his inner voice would alert him that "hey this girl hasn't been calling me".

This is why I said it earlier on, that you need to develop your inner sense of security and make it strong, because if it isn't, you would see yourself calling, checking up or stalking him.

Now that you're NOT blowing up his phone with 100 missed calls, you have given his imagination space to run wild, and men hate space. Men hate not having control of a situation, especially a man who has been using your emotions to make himself feel like King Kong.

After sometime, he would start to wonder why he isn't getting same reaction he usually gets from other girls from you. He would start thinking to himself, "was my D small?" ... "did I sleep with her, or was she the one that slept with me?" "Am I not the man here, how come she's not all panicky and all?"

Now, before he comes to you directly, he is going to try other means of finding out what you have been up to, he's going to start looking you up on your social media (WhatsApp status, Instagram, Snapchat, etc.) *Now he has turned to the stalker.*

Let me repeat it once again, it is important that you have an inner sense of security (You have to develop it my sister, 1 day at a time)

I want you to watch your self-talk, stop talking yourself down. Trust me you can control this whole situation and turn it around in your favor. I guarantee you that!

If you go uploading all those strong-girl quotes or you start putting up a social lifestyle just to get to him, he would most likely see through it and know that you are screaming for attention, which would inflate his ego instead of deflating it.

He wants to be significant; he desperately wants you to want him, and you getting back to your life like nothing happened means he is irrelevant. He won't be able to live with that. 9 out of 10 times, his ego would get the best of him.

Once you have him hooked here, you have total control over his ego once again, squeeze his emotional balls as much as you can (I'll explain this in detail, as you read on) Keep shocking him, until you have him all motivated and emotional about you again - just the way things were in the good old days before you gave him sex and he started thinking he was a boss.

I'm sure right now you're thinking - CAN'T I JUST BE NICE TO HIM? Nice kee you there! Is it not niceness that has landed you in this situation you're in right now? You already know human beings can be selfish when they see someone they can walk all over.

You're already giving him what he should only be getting from a relationship, without you both being in an actual relationship. Out of emotional hastiness, you are allowing him to get the benefits of a boyfriend, without the responsibility of being one and this is the very reason why he doesn't commit any further. You have given him enough chances to treat you how he wants, sometimes he can ignore your calls for 3 to 4 days, or he can forget your birthday and there's really nothing you do about it.

Do you now see the importance of giving him space at this point in time? You need to step back, create a vacuum and see how well he is going to fill up that gap.

In the game of persuasion and negotiation, there is something called *'The-walk-away-power'*. Everybody has this power in them, but you need self-confidence to be able to use it. Generally, in life, people would always try to treat you lesser than you deserve, and they watch to see if you would accept the nonsense treatment, they're giving you. If you smile and keep quiet, they simply continue treating you in that manner and adding more insult to the package every day. Stop allowing it. Activate your 'walk-away-power', you lose nothing by leaving!

If he acts indifferent or doesn't seem to care, the earlier you know the better. Some women ignore the reality of things, try managing the situation hoping it gets better. Well, I hope it gets better too, but reality is reality, and if you don't face it, eventually it will face you.

So, to answer the question -Can't I just be nice to him? The answer is NO! For now, you cannot be nice to him, until he comes back to his senses, and treats you like the Queen that you truly are.

So does this mean you should just be nasty and hateful towards him? - Of course not! You're NOT going to be nasty towards him, instead you're going to cover layers and layers of mean-ness, with a smooth layer of charming vibes and kindness. He won't know what hit him!

CHAPTER 7

WHAT MEN ~~WANT~~ NEED

The greatest weapon fashioned against a man's ego,
is a sweet charming woman,
who would not tolerate any of his bullshit!
- Atewo Laolu-Ogunniyi

Composure in a woman, weakens men! STAY COMPOSED!

In the world of men, there is no known strategy or defense mechanism, against a woman who is composed and who holds her shit together.

Men know that women have volatile emotions, they know women have very active minds. They also know the right or wrong things to say, to make a woman lose her senses, and this is how guys have played the game from the beginning of time.

A man would bring drama to you, then he would turn around and ask you "Why are you shouting?" or say "You're over-reacting"

He has done it for many girls before you and it worked, so this is the predictable reaction he expects to get from you, and he is getting it. Within the context of this book, when a man does this to you, he is only doing it to confirm that he still has EMOTIONAL CONTROL over you, he is enjoying the power he has over you, it caresses his ego like crazy.

Being COMPOSED does you a lot of good, because it helps you see the situation for what it really is. It gives you a better control of the situation.

I want you to think back to a time when you were provoked or manipulated by a guy that you liked. What was the main thing he kept using against you? I can bet he kept saying you were over-reacting, right?

That's the classic male behavior.

When a guy is not ready to attend to the problem you bring forward, he simply replaces it with another problem - Your Attitude!

I have seen situations, where a girl sees flirty messages on her man's phone and she confronts him about it. Only for the guy to flip the script and start making it look like she is being unnecessarily rude. Lo and behold, the girl starts apologizing for how-she-spoke-to-him instead of them actually speaking about the main issue itself.

A composed woman is never caught in this web of manipulation. She herself is a master at this game. She gives a man only two options. (1) - he either faces the problem, explain himself and apologize or (2) He shows his true color, that he is a fvckboy

He is not very used to a woman who composes herself, a woman who doesn't fall for his mental tricks, so he would lose balance in her presence. Once he plays all his games of reverse psychology and she doesn't flinch, he would start getting jittery.

The petty side of him would reveal itself and he might even go the extent of calling you names or insinuating that you have done something which you did not do.

This is the power of a composed woman; he would later turn around and come to apologize for his boyish behavior and this time his respect for you would have tripled.

This does not mean you are allowing him to walk all over you - NO! It simply means you are not letting him engage you in his emotionally-draining games

Now let me chip this in, because you want to be STRONG does not mean you should be HARDENED, and because you are SOFT does not mean you are weak.

Some women confuse being strong with being hardened. They are so hardened in their approach to life, that no man wants to stay long around them. Everything is fight, fight, fight. Everything is proving a point, prove a point.

But the truth is that they only run in the opposite direction of any situation that's requiring them to display their feminine side.

Never ever deny your femininity, if you do, you would be you lying to yourself about who you truly are, instead, learn to walk away from any man that tries to undervalue your femininity or tries to use it against you

I know this is not easy, and it might seem stressful, but this is the way you protect yourself from the contagious toxic games that fvckboys play.

A lady once told me that *"She's not fragile like an egg, she's fragile like a bomb!"* and I'm like "What's that?

Please don't be a bomb o! No man wants to put a bomb in the house. Even you yourself, do you want to have a bomb of a man as your husband? Remember you attract what you are, so if you are a bomb, it's most certain you will attract a bomb type-of-guy like yourself, both of you will now have an explosive relationship.

Looking at all of nature, we know that femininity is soft and tender, but this does not in any way mean that it is weak. I personally know that women are spirituality stronger and deeper (SOUL) than men. Men are only physically stronger (BODY).

When a woman's mind is plugged into a mission, she becomes more powerful and relentless than 10 men combined, this is why a woman go through the pains of giving birth and she would still get pregnant again and have another child. If it were men who were given the strenuous role of birthing babies, the world population would be less than 10 million people, most men would simply run away from the idea of having a second child or having any at all.

So never for a second think that being soft is the same as being weak, because it isn't.

Your strength exists in being yourself and walking away from any man that tries to devalue you.

WALKING AWAY, I repeat WALKING AWAY is the strength you need to learn how to activate, and I am sure you can see by now that, this is what this whole book is about.

If you are a feminine woman, who loves to be feminine, please stay that way. I am not telling you who to be, I am simply telling you to be yourself.

The more important battle here is between you and those your emotions that come in a rush.

Let's take a look at some of 'THOSE EMOTIONS'

Those emotions that always push you to want to call and talk about things, even when you clearly know he would not say anything sensible in the phone conversation.

Those emotions that make you keep going out of your way to care for him even after you can clearly see that he is changing and he is acting up.

Those emotions that make you blame yourself for something you didn't do,

Those emotions that influence you to keep making excuses for him e.g. "Maybe I should have been more understanding" "Maybe he was truly going through a hard time"

Your grip of the situation starts from having control over these emotions, because that is what he is using to confuse your whole being. Learn to control these emotions, learn to push them into the background, learn to deprive yourself of that short-term satisfaction of hearing his voice.

You don't learn it in a day, so please don't rush yourself, but by reading this book up to this point, you are now more conscious of it.

Anytime you feel that rush coming over you, pick this book up and read this part to yourself as a reminder of what you should not be doing.

The fact is, a man cannot take advantage of you, if you don't stay and keep condoning the bullshit over and over again.

CHAPTER 8

TURN THE DAMN TABLE!

*When dealing with a changing man,
not being scared of losing him,
is your best shot at having him.*
- Atewo Laolu-Ogunniyi

1) **MENTAL SPACE -** Would make him idealize you all over again, just the way he used to do, before he got all familiar with you and started thinking he has seen all of you.

2) **PHYSICAL SPACE/DISTANCE -** They say absence makes the heart fonder. This is what a calm but lethal dose of physical space would do to him.

To give a person space, the very first things you stop doing, is the frequent calling and random check-up, stop following every urge to ask him how his day was, or to show him you care at every chance. He knows you care already, there's nothing to prove there anymore. What you need to show him now, is that caring is a two-people thing and one person cannot do all the caring alone.

Decrease the intimacy and affection, don't *delete* it, just decrease it to a very noticeable level. You have to subtract the sex too; it has to be put aside for a while. If you give a man all the space in the world -but you're always ready to open your legs for him when he calls - you won't be getting your point across.

Have a short heart-to-heart talk with him, tell him you feel its best the sex stops, while you continue being friends. What you are basically doing here is that you're sending him back to the friend-zone and no man likes to be in that zone of torture. As *calmly* as possible, without talking too much or over-flogging the matter, let him see that nothing is going to change your mind. Now has new reasons to win you over again.

Make sure you do this as *maturely* as possible. Men are defenceless when a woman is CALM BUT FIRM. Before you know it, he would be all over you begging again. As I mentioned before, all he wants is to distract you from your daily life, and make himself the centre of your attention. The more you fuss over him, the more he is happy that he has that much power over you. If you are not moved from your centre point, he would then keep trying and trying till he eventually falls.

There will just be this attitude of indifference about you, like you don't really care if he is there or not. Yet, whenever you both talk on phone, you're still as nice and as graceful as ever, with no nag in your voice.

The mixed signals of your actions would baffle him. No longer do you complain or say things like - *'oh I called you, you didn't call back'* or say things like *'do you miss me?*

If he calls after 5 days, you pick the phone and speak like you didn't even notice that he hasn't been calling. You're not playing games here, you're only putting him in his place, and you're also learning how to not let an inconsistent guy consume your emotional energy.

When he sees that you're not whining or complaining, he would start playing the blame-game. He would dare to accuse you of not calling him, and say something like "Do you know what I have been going through these past few days? You didn't even bother to call me"

DRAMA ALERT! My sister, do not engage him, I repeat do not engage him!

His mission is to tease you, piss you off, make you lose it and then hang up the phone on you after confirming he still has emotional control over you.

Just chuckle and nicely say "Eeyah sorry o, I hope you've sorted things out now"

Now you have become undefinable, something beyond his understanding. You are now a mystery he would be craving to unravel, a puzzle he needs to solve. If you get control of the situation to this point (and I know you can), he would keep pondering over your actions, till you completely take over his imagination. A man doesn't imagine or fantasize about what we he sees in front of him, he only imagines those things that he doesn't see. So to get into his mind, you need to get out of his face.

I hope you're fully with me, and you're getting a clearer picture - Good!

The fact that you're always being too-available and ready to compromise, has not been working in your favor. Take back control of the situation now, and don't even be scared that he would run away. Cast that fear out of your mind now!

Now if you find that you slip and somehow you landed on his penis again, don't try to make him feel guilty for doing something he didn't force you to do, he only played your emotions to his favour.

You can lie to me, but don't lie to yourself, maybe conji (hornyness) was catching you too - so you allowed yourself to believe his sweet words till you ended up in his room, under his duvet.

I'm not judging you, but you now need to get a grip on yourself, own your emotions, and turn the damn tables. Play his emotions to your favour too.

Don't go petty and start using sex against him, or assume he owes you some kind of affectionate payback - No. That's becoming a relationship of emotional buying and selling, where you trade sex for love, and that can only last as far as the next orgasm goes.

Sex won't keep a man. If you like give him spider-man style and somersaulting doggy, he would only keep coming back for the sexual act and not for you!

You can't be giving him sweet love-making while he's only using you to masturbate. Feeding him your body while you starve your heart? - Error!

Don't let him draw you into his petty game of emotional hide and seek, where he is nice today, and moody tomorrow. Step back into your lane, stand your ground, he would come to you sooner than you think.

Giving a guy 'space' does not mean being nasty or dramatic. You are not changing who you are, you are only reserving it. You are not nasty you are nice - only that, your niceness is set aside for those who deserve it. Those who don't deserve it would only get an attitude of indifference from you, and with the way he has been behaving lately, he falls into the category people who don't deserve your niceness.

You are not complex, you have simply gone from being that 'easy to predict' girl, to a mystery he must unravel.

CHAPTER 9

WHAT IF...

Don't burn daylight chasing the wrong one,
The right one won't run
- Dr Phil

WHAT IF I GIVE HIM SPACE AND HE GOES?

A man would never ever leave a woman he wants, just because she gave him space.

Men are born-hunters, his manly nature and his ego, would not let him drift away - NEVER! Drama and pressure can make a man leave, but not space.

In the beginning he was giving you attention and doing things to blow your mind - right? So it's one of two things, It's either he behaved that way just to get sex from you, or he actually had feelings and still has feelings for you, but then out of over familiarity a.k.a *see finish,* those feelings faded into the background.

Either way, you need to find out what's going on, and you need to find out now! Do not postpone the day you face reality, do not cut yourself with a blunt knife!

The worst that can happen is that he would go, but taking the action by yourself to know exactly where you stand, would help you grow as a person, it means you take charge of what happens to you.

There are 2 types of pain in life, the pain of discipline and the pain of regret.

The Pain of Discipline means you happen to life, you command respect and dictate how you let people treat you. This tremendously helps you grow as a person.

The Pain of Regret occurs when you let life happen to you, you allow people to use and treat you as they please. This must stop!

Of course, you cannot control every single incident that happens around you, but you can sure control how you respond to every single situation. No one can take that power from you.

They say 'when things are not adding up, subtract yourself', the pain you get from removing yourself from an unhealthy association is the Pain Of Discipline and it matures you, but if you decide to ignore the signs, and stick around till life happens, that would be the pain of regret, and it can make a person feel stupid .

Don't carry a mountain you are supposed to climb over, don't let something that's supposed to be a paragraph in your life be a chapter. Sometimes we unnecessarily beat ourselves up, over the fact that someone doesn't want a relationship with us at a particular place and time. But hey, we are all experiencing different stages of life at different times.

The fact that someone doesn't want commitment with you at a time, is not about you, it's about them, it doesn't mean you are not good enough. The other person, could have had bad relationships they haven't quite gotten over, he might be planning to achieve some goals at that point in time, and might feel commitment can distract him. That's why it's good to identify from the onset, if the person you are hooking up with, wants the same thing as you want. And if they don't, don't feel dejected! Don't ever feel dejected! Pick yourself up and move on, let your strong sense of self-worth guide you.

Now what if he has feelings for you, but he is just sleeping (emotionally), then wake him up! Get out from under his grip! Display that attitude of indifference! It's time for you to go to sleep too (emotionally). In his quest to have you in the palm of his hand again, he would come out into the open, off-guard, and there you have your catch!

WHAT IF ANOTHER GIRL GIVES HIM ATTENTION WHILE I'M AWAY?

Yes, it's possible, it's possible another girl gives him attention, while you are serving him space, or he could even go out to search for her attention himself. Whatever the case, she is a new flame. She is probably just another eye candy. You just stay in your own lane, its high time you let him realize that you are more than just an object of physical attraction, you know what you want, and if he is not going to give you the love you want, without a doubt, someone better would come along and give it to you.

As I mentioned earlier it's all *'see finish'* (over familiarity), he has seen you without your wig, he has seen you without your make up. He is now running an unfair comparison; he is comparing your own behind the scenes to the new girl's final package after filters and all. Let him do as pleases, you just make sure you don't struggle for his attention. You're not a proud girl, you are a principled woman.

Of course, I'm not saying you should hide the fact that you still have feelings for him, but right now you can't be too emotionally open with him. Instead, you let him see that even though you might have a soft spot for him, you would still hold your ground.

He has been taking your kindness for a weakness, he has been taking advantage of the fact that you like him. When he sees that he cannot feed his ego off your desperation any longer, he would start to respect you all over again, and naturally, a man is drawn to what he respects.

Note though, you do not get respect by putting up a strong face, or raising your voice unnecessarily - NO. You cannot force respect, rather you command respect. You earn it by first respecting yourself.

SHOULD I CALL HIM TO TALK ABOUT IT?

Are you kidding me? You still want to call him and talk? Are you a parrot? Don't even make me laugh right now. If you like call him and sing, his ego is not making him hear what you are saying. It's not talk-time anymore, now it's SHOW TIME!

Here are 10 reasons why you shouldn't call him back. I want you to read these 10 reasons twice

1) The signs don't lie. If a man values you, he wouldn't be treating you this way

2) It's up to you to make him respect and value you, but chasing him up and down is not the way to go about it.

3) The MORE YOU TALK, THE LESS HE HEARS - You've asked all the questions, given all the explanations. It's no longer about what you say, it's now about what you don't say.

4) WORDS MEOW, ACTIONS ROAR - Your actions would reinforce your value more than your words ever would.

5) He's feeding his ego off your desperation - LEAN BACK!

6) You're not wrong for falling for him, but you'll be careless if you keep on falling after all his nonchalant vibes.

7) Stop getting excited 'too quickly' when he calls out-of-the-blue, he just wants you on his heels again.

8) Now you're thinking, maybe you just love him too much - NOPE! YOU DON'T LOVE HIM TOO MUCH, YOU JUST LOVE YOURSELF TOO LITTLE.

9) IT'S NOT EASY, I know. But he is not your problem. Falling for him is not your problem. Your problem is that little voice in your head that's not saying the right things.

10) DON'T BE SCARED TO FACE REALITY and whatever it brings. It is never as painful as your fears make you think it'll be. Grab the bull by the horns, your-future-self would thank you for it.

Your emotions are not always your best friends, and you have to start learning how to have a certain level of control over them. I am not saying you should deny them, that would mean you are not telling yourself the truth, I am saying you should start controlling them and not them (your emotions) controlling you.

You say ignoring him is not easy, as you have grown so fond of him lately, and he has become part of your every-day. But the truth is that, its not the act of 'ignoring him' that's hard for you to do, controlling your emotions is the thing that's hard.

If you keep allowing your emotions to run helter-skelter, it's going to be tearing you apart. I know it is not easy, but that's adulthood for you. Nothing comes easy. No pain no gain!

If you allow your inner emotions to over-run, just know that **uncontrolled emotions create baseless sentiments**. You would see yourself tolerating shit you should never tolerate e.g. - *"oh, he didn't pick his phone for a whole week, despite seeing all my missed calls and messages, well maybe he was really busy as he said"*. That is ridiculous, but it happens a lot, when your emotions have developed six packs and are stronger than you.

And it's not only girls it happens to, it happens to guys too, it has happened to me personally, when I was in uni, there was this girl I was crazy about, and she was crazy about me too, but somewhere along the line, one of her ex-toasters came back from London and started confusing her. I was priority before, I just suddenly realized I was becoming the option. I had typhoid - straight! My mum took me to the hospital, the doctors checked me, they didn't see any typhoid. But I was running a high temperature and shaking. Then my elder brother told the girl I wasn't feeling fine, so she sent me a text like this - *"Hey baby, I heard you aren't feeling too good, I'm so sorry, I would come check you up as soon as I can. Get better for me".* After reading her message, it didn't take 30 seconds for the typhoid to leave my body, forever!

So honestly it happens to everybody, don't grant yourself the short-term satisfaction of hearing his voice or stalking his every move, but on the other end you are creating a long-term problem of emotional pain for yourself.

CHAPTER 10

BEWARE OF HIS REVERSE-PSYCHOLOGY

He needs to know
He still has control over you,
And if you don't let him know,
He'll try to make you feel bad for doing so.
- Atewo Laolu-Ogunniyi

B y now he is baffled at the way you are handling the whole situation. His man-liness is under attack by this cool-distant attitude you just put up.

One part of him knows you are a nice girl, because he has seen the nice part of you before. What he doesn't understand is this other part of you he is seeing. *What kind of girl is this?* - he thinks.

Is there some other guy in her life? He stalks you, both online and in real life, he sees that there's no other guy, so he keeps on wondering what could be wrong. *Wasn't she in love with me just a short while ago?*

Men have this belief, both from nature and from social-nurturing that - The man is always in control, so this lack of control over you, is really making him go gaga. How can this be happening?

So he uses one last tactic to disarm you and get control over you again. He activates operation REVERSE PSYCHOLOGY.

There are different ways men use reverse psychology. He could say, he was going through a hard time at work or in his business and he only wanted you to be more understanding, but since you acted this way, you have destroyed the chances of both of you building a relationship together.

He could say he had some sensitive family issues to solve and instead of you being there to be his only support-system, you also decided to turn against him.

Basically, he would try to flip it on you and make it look like you have just been selfish and you're only thinking of yourself. This is when you need to playback the days when you kept calling and checking up on him. All the dates and nights-out that he stood you up and cancelled plans on you at the last minute, without giving a proper explanation.

This is why I called this chapter - Beware of his REVERSE PSYCHOLOGY, because the emotional woman in you, would nearly break at this point, even though you know deep down in your soul that he is making up excuses.

Don't forget, that you have not been mean or nasty to him, so there is absolutely no justification for these things he his saying. You have only stepped back into the lane of yourself worth, and that is NOT something he usually gets with other women. He is used to always having his way.

I know you really like him, and you wish everything would just flow normally. But like I said much earlier, you cannot start to fully show a guy how much you need him, when his ego and selfishness is still bigger than the love, he feels for you. (Even parents are not always open with their children. When they need to discipline the child, they intentionally withdraw some benefits for the meantime)

I need you to understand what I'm about to say now. When he tries to use reverse psychology on you, do not allow yourself to get infuriated or angry. Don't! That's exactly the reaction he wants from you, so don't give him. He brings drama your way, says a few things to make you flare up, and when you do flare up, he laughs and gets on his way, leaving you to wish you had reacted in a different way.

Next thing you're texting him, telling him you both need to see and talk... TABLES TURNED AGAIN! Like I said earlier, *you're in the game already, so play and play good.*

Allow him to be deceiving himself, you are not about that old school mind game anymore. Hold yourself in a higher esteem than that which he is offering you. You definitely know what a man should do if he truly wants you.

Do not be the woman a man wants, rather be the woman a man NEEDS.

When a man wants you, he can easily outgrow the desires he once had for you. Then he would start looking around for another woman that can also satisfy his 'desires or want'

But when a man needs you, it means you have commanded more respect from him than he has ever had to give a woman and you don't do this by working on him, you do it by working on yourself and not allowing him to offer you his narcissistic treatment.

Men don't offer you bullshit in big sizes, they do it little by little, in tiny inches. The more bad behavior you allow him to get away with, the more bullshit he would offer you next time. Until one day you just look around and realize you don't have a voice in the relationship anymore and people close to you would be asking you why you allow him to treat you the way he does, and you wouldn't even be able to explain.

Apply the timeless principles in this book, and you would inevitably become a **CALMER**, **STRONGER** and more **FOCUSED WOMAN**! The exact type of woman every man dreams of!

THE END!

Printed in Great Britain
by Amazon

36780259R00051